THE CAPTIVITY OF
THE LOST SOUL

An Inspiration from The Book of Acts of the Apostles 26:17-18

by

FREDERICK AMON-ARMAH
(A-A FREDDY)

Foreword By

REV. BONIFACE KEELSON

Dedicated To

EVANGELIST REINHARD BONNKE
of blessed memory

GFIOM Publication @ 2020

God's Finger International Outreach Ministry
P. O. Box KF2188
Eastern Region
Ghana
Tel: +233 246 055 262 OR +233 55 780 9190
Email: *tfgiom@rocketmail.com*

This Book Is Dedicated To The Late

EVANGELIST REINHARD BONNKE

Who Has Much Impacted My Life And Ministry From Afar

And To All Soul Winners

ACKNOWLEDGEMENT

I am immensely grateful to God for the inspiration given me to write this booklet.

My thanks to my wife, Diana Amon-Armah, for her love and encouragement. I am also most grateful to two great brothers in the Lord, Pastor Felix Osei Amoateng (Administrator of God's Finger International Outreach Ministry [GFIOM]) and Jethro Apeawini Datamwin (Prayer Director of GFIOM) for their contributions in writing this little piece. I also thank Rev. Dr. Emmanuel Odame Obuobi (Eastern Region C Superintendent of Assemblies of God, Ghana) who inspires me much with his great teachings of the word of God.

Lastly but not least to Rev. Boniface Keelson, (a great mentor) for writing the foreword to this book.

God bless you richly.

FOREWORD

The Captivity of the Lost Soul is the fascinating title of Frederick Amon-Armah's new book. The book is basically about making extra effort to win the unsaved at all cost. Drawing lessons from Apostle Paul's testimony of his conversion in Acts 26:17-18, Evangelist Amon-Armah spells out that the unsaved is caged and kept in bondage by the devil. Frederick concludes that for meaningful and effective soul winning, believers must engage in warfare prayers on the behalf of the unsaved.

The firebrand Evangelist whose passion and pursuit for more than a decade has been soul winning through crusades, outreaches and revivals, maintains that "Winning the Unsaved" is nothing less than a spiritual warfare. This simple and precisely outlined book is a great eye opener to all who desire to get the lost saved. I feel this book is the tonic stimulant we need in the church for our soul winning effort.

My prayer is that the Holy Spirit shall give you deeper insight as you acquire new knowledge on winning the unsaved from this book.

Shalom!
REV. BONIFACE KEELSON
Snr Pastor/Missionary/Evangelist,
Lighthouse Assembly of God, Toronto, Canada.

CONTENT

ACKNOWLEDGEMENT iv

FOREWORD v

INTRODUCTION 1

BACKGROUND TO THE BOOK OF ACTS 8

JESUS DESCRIBES THE CAPTIVITY OF THE LOST SOUL 10
   SIX CHARACTERISTICS OF THE LOST SOUL 15
      Figurative Expressions 15
      Literal Expressions 18

A CALL TO EVANGELISM 24

SPIRITUAL WARFARE 26
   LIVING AS JESUS LIVED 31
   MAKING WARFARE THROUGH PRAYER FOR THE LOST 32
      Martin Boos 33
      Daniel Nash and Charles Finney 34
      John Knox 36
      John Wesley 36
      Reinhard Bonnke 36
   PREACHING THE GOSPEL 43

ABOUT THE BOOK 45

HOW TO PARTNER WITH US 49

INTRODUCTION

Mankind is God's treasured creation; made in His own image. Being full of the wisdom and nature of God, man was a proud inhabitant of God's kingdom and a caretaker of other creatures as assigned to him by the Almighty God. Adam, a complete representative of the human race was a royal of the kingdom of God and had eternal fellowship with God. Even though he was a handiwork of God, he was endowed with one greatest power, thus, the will power.

However, the devil (satan) managed to deceive man to commit a high treason against God. Man believed satan and contradicted instructions by God. All mankind (represented in Adam) willfully and unknowingly handed over authority as ruler of the world to satan who now rules and controls the dark world. Man lost his rightful and original place in the kingdom of God. This was the beginning of the doom and captivity of man.

Man lost sonship, fellowship and the nature of God, hence, became a lost soul. Man became dead to God (spiritually dead) and a slave in the kingdom of satan, thus, exalting the works of the flesh (Galatians 5:19-21, Proverbs 6:6-19). Sin and selfishness became the nature of man. Man lost the light of God and satan flooded the heart of men with darkness (Jeremiah 17:9).

> *The acts of the flesh are obvious: sexual immorality, impurity and debauchery; idolatry and witchcraft; hatred, discord, jealousy, fits of rage, selfish ambition, dissensions, factions and envy; drunkenness, orgies, and the like. I warn you, as I did before, that those who live like this will not inherit the kingdom of God. ~ Galatians 5:19-21 New International Version (NIV)*

There are six things the Lord hates, seven that are detestable to him: haughty eyes, a lying tongue, hands that shed innocent blood, a heart that devises wicked schemes, feet that are quick to rush into evil, a false witness who pours out lies and a person who stirs up conflict in the community. ~ Proverbs 6:16-19 New International Version (NIV)

"The heart is deceitful above all things, and desperately wicked; Who can know it? ~ Jeremiah 17:9 New King James Version (NKJV)

The lost man, thus, enjoys wickedness over mercy, hatred over love, pride over humility, fame over simplicity, and selfishness and greed over empathy and selfless sacrifice.

Our Lord Jesus Christ himself described the captivity of the lost soul (man) to Apostle Paul as under the control of the satanic world. Before his encounter with the Lord Jesus, the soul of Paul who was then called Saul was flooded with darkness. Nonetheless, glory to God, on his was to Damascus to persecute believers, he encountered the Lord of all (Acts 9:3-4), the light of the world (John 8:12), the sun in heaven and the radiance of God's glory (Hebrews 1:3), thus, our Lord Jesus Christ. For the light of God shines and darkness cannot overcome it (John 1:5), so the darkness that flooded Saul's soul instantly disappeared upon his encounter with the Lord Jesus Christ. Saul was delivered from the captivity of satan so that he could also cause the deliverance of others who were lost. He was liberated from being a slave of satan so that he could in turn cause the liberation of others from satan (Acts 26:17).

Beloved, like Apostle Paul, the day we encountered Christ, we were rescued from the kingdom of satan. We were liberated from the nature of the devil to exhibit the nature of God. We were liberated from filthy lives into holy lives (Hebrews 13:12). We were liberated from the power of sin unto the power of God's righteousness. We were liberated from demonic sicknesses and diseases into divine health and wellness. We were liberated from gloom into glory (2 Corinthians 3:18), from failure into excellence (2 Corinthians 4:7), from eternal death into eternal life (John 3:16), from the power of darkness into the power of God's mighty light (Matthew 5:14). We were liberated from imperfection into perfection and from corruptible into incorruptible (1 Peter 1:23). We were liberated from fulling satanic mandate into fulfilling God's divine mandate and assignment. In a nut shell we have been liberated to liberate others.

Until a person experiences liberty, he or she cannot bring others to experience liberty. The liberator has to get what it takes to liberate the captives. Moses had to leave Egypt before he could lead the people of Israel out of Egypt. Our Lord and saviour Jesus Christ had to become sin and overcome sin and its power before He could liberate those who turn to Him from sin (Hebrews 5:8-9).

> *Though He was a Son, yet He learned obedience by the things which He suffered. And having been perfected, He became the author of eternal salvation to all who obey Him ~ Hebrews 5:7-9 New King James Version (NKJV)*

We need to understand the problems of those who are still bound by the devil in order to cause their liberation. Apostle Paul needed to understand the captivity of the lost souls to whom he was being sent (Acts 26:17).

> *I will deliver you from the Jewish people, as well as from the Gentiles,* **to whom I now send you** *~ Acts 26:17 New King James Version (NKJV).*

Knowing how to swim does not guarantee that you can save those who are sinking. When you understand how a sinking man feels and will act if you try to save him, you will know exactly what to do to save him. Many believers approach evangelism from a very carnal mindset. Without much spiritual and physical investments, and preparation, they venture the field of souls and realize a poor outcome. Though the harvest is plentiful, the labourers are few (Matthew 9:37). Not only are they few but there are also few passionate and skilled labourers. I believe this book will contribute to knowledge on soul winning, hence, enlighten and empower believers in our rescue mission - the great commission. The following pages exposes the book of Acts chapter 26 verses 17 to 18 concerning the captivity of the lost soul, the need for intercession for the lost and the preaching of the gospel to the lost.

1

BACKGROUND TO THE BOOK OF ACTS

The book of Acts was written by Luke who was a gentile physician and historian to Theophilus. He wrote this book between AD 63 and 70 to give account of what happened to the disciples and followers of our Lord Jesus Christ, and the birth and growth of the Christian church. Luke told Theophilus how the gospel spread from Jerusalem to Samaria, and finally other parts of the earth by the Holy Spirit empowering believers to witness of the Lordship of Jesus Christ. Thus, the endurance and the growth of the church in spite of the persecutions and oppositions of the times. Though the identity of Theophilus was not emphatically mentioned, many theologians have stated that Theophilus was perhaps a sympathetic Roman ruler, but still pagan, whom Luke was endeavoring to persuade of the truth of the gospel.

2

JESUS DESCRIBES THE CAPTIVITY OF THE LOST SOUL

TEXT: Acts 26:17-18 New International Version (NIV)

> *I will rescue you from your own people and from the Gentiles. I am sending you to them to open their eyes and turn them from darkness to light, and from the power of Satan to God, so that they may receive forgiveness of sins and a place among those who are sanctified by faith in me.*

The theme of the writer of the book of Acts was to recommend the evidences of the Christian faith to the official Roman world as represented in Theophilus. Similarly, Paul the Apostle in Acts chapter 26 sought to remind his audience that the gentiles had equal share in

God's inheritance if only they would believe in Jesus Christ and surrender to him. He shared his testimony on how God delivered and saved him, changing him from a passionate persecutor of the church to a sacrosanct preacher of the gospel.

Prior to this opportunity, Paul was falsely accused in Jerusalem of bringing a Gentile into the temple (which to the Jews was a dishonor to the temple) for which reason the Jews arrested him (Acts 24:5-6).

> "We have found this man to be a troublemaker, stirring up riots among the Jews all over the world. He is a ringleader of the Nazarene sect and even tried to desecrate the temple; so we seized him. ~ Acts 24:5-6 New International Version (NIV)

A crowd dragged Paul out the temple and beat him until a leader of the Roman cohort arrived with soldiers and centurions, who intervened (Acts 21:30-32).

> *The whole city was aroused, and the people came running from all directions. Seizing Paul, they dragged him from the temple, and immediately the gates were shut. While they were trying to kill him, news reached the commander of the Roman troops that the whole city of Jerusalem was in an uproar. He at once took some officers and soldiers and ran down to the crowd. When the rioters saw the commander and his soldiers, they stopped beating Paul. ~ Acts 21:30-32 New International Version (NIV)*

Paul was arrested but was given opportunity to talk to the crowd about his conversion and how the Lord sent him to the gentiles because the Jews wouldn't accept his testimony (Acts 22:1-22). Paul was imprisoned and tried before the Sanhedrin where he created confusion among them declaring that he was a Pharisee (Acts 23:1-10). The night after, the Lord appeared to Paul to comfort him and asked him to testify also in Rome (Acts 23:11).

> *The following night the Lord stood near Paul and said, "Take courage! As you have testified about me in Jerusalem, so you must also testify in Rome."* ~ *Acts 23:11 New International Version (NIV)*

The next morning more than forty Jews conspired to kill Paul but their plans were exposed (Acts 23:12-35). As a result, Paul was sent to Caesarea where he spent two years in prison before he was sent to Rome for a trial before Romans and Jews (Acts 25). In Acts 26, Agrippa who was one of the Roman-appointed rulers in Israel was asked by Festus who had succeeded Felix as governor in Caesarea to advice on Paul's case. Paul recounted how Jesus changed his life.

As Paul made his speech in Acts 26, he got to a point where he narrated how he met Christ and what message Christ gave him (Acts 26: 16-18). It is from Christ's message to Paul that I deduce the Captivity of the lost soul. The lost soul has many problems for which Christ commissioned Paul as a solution carrier.

Apostle Paul mentioned that Christ said to him "*I am sending you to them to **open their eyes** and **turn them from darkness to light**, and **from the power of Satan to God**, so that they may **receive forgiveness of sins** and **a place** among those who are **sanctified by faith** in me.*"

Acts 26: 17-18 mentions 6 characteristics of the lost soul. Jesus uses two figurative expressions and four literal expressions to describe the captivity of the people to whom he was sending Paul.

SIX CHARACTERISTICS OF THE LOST SOUL

Figurative Expressions

1) The lost are blind

Jesus said to Paul that he was sending him to open their eyes—

In this context "open their eyes" is used figuratively to denote spiritual blindness of souls that are lost, though they may not be physically blind. This blindness refers to their inability to see the glory of the good news and to understand the message of the gospel. This blindness is caused by satan.

> *2 Corinthians 4:4 (NLT) states that "Satan, who is the god of this world, has **blinded** the minds of those who don't believe. They are **unable to see** the glorious light of the Good News. They **don't understand** this message about*

the glory of Christ, who is the exact likeness of God."

2) The lost are darkness and live in darkness

Jesus said to Paul that he was sending him to turn them from darkness to light—

Our Lord Jesus Christ uses the word darkness also figuratively to imply that the lost soul is spiritually darkness and also lives in darkness. In Ephesians 5:8 we are made to understand that we were formerly darkness, but now are Light in the Lord; thus we should walk as children of Light.

*For **you were once darkness**, but now you are light in the Lord. Live as children of light ~ Ephesians 5:8 New International Version (NIV)*

Greater Love Miracle Campaign (GLMC) at Tolon, Northern Region of Ghana.

1 Peter 2:9 states that we as believers have been called out of darkness into Christ's marvelous light.

> *But you are a chosen people, a royal priesthood, a holy nation, God's special possession, that you may declare the praises of him who called you out of **darkness into his wonderful light**. ~ 1 Peter 2:9 New International Version (NIV)*

Literal Expressions

3) The lost are under the power of satan

Jesus said to Paul that he was sending him to turn them from the power of Satan unto God—

This is literal such that one cannot serve two masters (Matthew 6:24). It is either a person is submitted and lives under the power of God through our Lord Jesus or a person is submitted and lives under the power of Satan. Ephesians 2:1-2 teaches us that, prior to our salvation, we were under the power of satan and controlled by him.

> *As for you, you were dead in your transgressions and sins, in which you used to live when you followed the ways of this world and of the ruler of the kingdom of the air, the spirit who is now at work in those who are disobedient. ~ Ephesians 2:1-2 New International Version (NIV)*

4) The lost are in need of forgiveness

So that they may receive forgiveness of sins—

The lost soul is a sinner, living in sin and whose sins are not forgiven. It is only by confessing that a person can be forgiven. 1 John 1:9 says if we confess our sins, he is faithful and just to forgive us our sins and to cleanse us from all unrighteousness. But how can the lost soul know or realize this truth if he has not heard the message of the gospel through which the Holy Spirit will convict of sin, righteousness and of judgment (John 16:8).

> "How shall they call on Him in whom they have not believed? And how shall they believe in Him of whom they have not heard? And how shall they hear without a preacher? And how shall they preach unless they are sent? As it is written: "How beautiful are the feet of those who preach

the gospel of peace, Who bring glad tidings of good things!" ~ Romans 10:14-15 New International Version (NIV)

5) The lost have no inheritance in God

And *a place among those* who are sanctified by faith in me—

The lost soul has no inheritance in God among the saints. They have no place in the kingdom of God until they experience the new birth (1 Peter 1:3-4) by believing in their hearts and confessing with their mouths that God raised Christ from the dead (Romans 10:9).

> *1 Peter 1:3-4 says our God in his great mercy has given us new birth into a living hope through the resurrection of Jesus Christ from the dead, and into an inheritance that can never perish, spoil*

or fade. This inheritance is kept in heaven for us.

If you declare with your mouth, "Jesus is Lord," and believe in your heart that God raised him from the dead, you will be saved. ~ Romans 10:9 New International Version (NIV)

6) The Lost are not sanctified

Among those *who are **sanctified by faith in me** –*

The lost soul is not sanctified because they do not have faith in Christ Jesus. The blood of Jesus cannot cleanse the sins of the lost when they have not confessed their sins and accepted Jesus Christ as their Lord and Saviour. In their ignorance the lost think they are ok without Christ. They think by following a set of rules made by man and being nice and kind to people makes then sanctified. They think that, by not inflicting pain on others makes them sanctified. However, nothing makes a man sanctified except the blood of Jesus Christ (Hebrews 10:10) through the working of the Holy Spirit (2 Thessalonians 2:13; 1 Peter 1:2) when we believe in Jesus Christ (2 Thessalonians 2:13).

> *And by that will, we have been made holy (sanctified) through the sacrifice of the body of Jesus Christ once for all.* ~ Hebrews 10:10

/New International Version (NIV)

> *Who have been chosen according to the foreknowledge of God the Father, through the sanctifying work of the Spirit, to be obedient to Jesus Christ and sprinkled with his blood: Grace and*

peace be yours in abundance. ~ 1 Peter 1:2 New International Version (NIV)

But we ought always to thank God for you, brothers and sisters loved by the Lord, because God chose you as first fruits to be saved through the sanctifying work of the Spirit and through belief in the truth. ~ 2 Thessalonians 2:13 New International Version (NIV)

Was paralyzed in bed but healed and dancing to the Glory of God at GLMC, Tolon

3

A CALL TO EVANGELISM

The captivity of the people from whom Paul was called out and those of the Gentiles, seems to be a reason for which Paul was sent out. By Paul's submission and obedience to Christ, these people would receive deliverance and salvation. If Paul preaches the gospel to them and they believed, their eyes would be open, they would be turned into light, they would come under the power of God our father, their sins would be forgiven, they would have a place or inheritance in Christ among the saints and they would be sanctified. These are all-in-one instantaneous rather than chronological processes that goes on in a man's life when they receive Christ Jesus our Lord upon hearing the gospel.

As the Lord Jesus Christ called Paul, this same instantaneous process of deliverance and salvation was manifested in his life. Much the same way, when we confessed with our mouths unto salvation and believed with our hearts unto righteousness, we also experienced this process. Like Paul was called out and sent out, we have also been called out and sent out by our Lord Jesus to our families, clans, villages, communities, towns and nations to preach the message of the gospel to open the eyes of the lost souls, and turn them from darkness to light, and from the power of Satan to God, so that they may receive forgiveness of sins and a place among us who are sanctified by faith in Christ Jesus.

4

SPIRITUAL WARFARE

Soul winning is spiritual and it is warfare. God our father has done his part by sending his son Jesus Christ in the fullness of time. So the Scripture mentions in Galatians 4:4-5, that;

> .....when the set time had fully come, God sent his Son, born of a woman, born under the law, to redeem those under the law, that we might **receive adoption** to sonship... (NIV).

Nonetheless, it takes those who have been saved to act as catalyst to the salvation of others. We have been saved to bring others to be saved. Jesus intercedes for us (Romans 8:34) and we are to interceded for the lost.

> *Who then is the one who condemns? No one. Christ Jesus who died--more than that, who was raised to life--is at the right hand of God and is also **interceding for us**. ~ Romans 8:34*
> *–New International Version (NIV)*

Note that, Galatians 4:5 says **that we might receive adoption**.... God has given but the reception lies in the will of men. How can they receive when they are blind to see what has been given? How can they receive when they are bound in darkness? How can the receive when they are under the power of Satan (meaning their will power has been compromised, and are being controlled and governed by the kingdom of darkness)? How can they receive adoption into sonship when their minds are manipulated, their hearts captured and controlled, and their hands and legs bound by Satan and his cohorts?

Cross section of crusade audience at Tolon, Northern Region, Ghana

Your salvation and my salvation are results of prayers and intercessions made by some saved men and women who may still be alive or even dead. Our ability to receive and not neglect or ignore the great salvation was because someone's lifestyle and prayer brought light and liberty to us, such that, as the word was preached or ministered to us, we saw and had the ability to receive.

Note the sequence in which our Lord Jesus states this to Apostle Paul, *I am sending you to them to 1)* ***open their eyes*** *and 2)* ***turn them from darkness to light,*** *and 3)* ***from the power of Satan to God,*** <u>***SO THAT THEY MAY RECEIVE***</u>. The first three conditions; the opening of their eyes, the turning from darkness into light and from the power of satan unto God is to enable them receive the next three conditions. SO THAT THEY MAY RECEIVE *1) forgiveness of sins, 2) a place or an inheritance 3) and sanctification by faith in Christ Jesus.*

I have seen highly demon possessed people struggle to confess Jesus Christ as their Lord and savior. They had to go through deliverance through warfare on their behalf, before they had the will to confess Jesus as Lord and asked for forgiveness.

To reach out to men to bring them to the saving knowledge of our Lord Jesus, we need to engage in warfare employing our spiritual weapons.

> *For the weapons of our warfare are not carnal but mighty in God for pulling down strongholds, casting down arguments and every high thing that exalts itself against the knowledge of God, bringing every thought into captivity to the obedience of Christ, and being ready to punish all disobedience when your obedience is fulfilled. 2 Corinthians 10:4-6 (NKJV)*

Our weapons in this warfare are in three folds.

A. The brightening of our light through living as our Lord Jesus Christ did and has commanded us.

B. Employing the weapon of prayer on behalf of the lost souls.

C. Preaching the message of gospel.

Let's elaborate these further.

LIVING AS JESUS LIVED

We are to live as Christ lived because, Jesus our Lord himself is our life according to Colossians 3:4. As he is, so are we here in this world (1 John 4:17). He is the light of the world (John 8:12). In John 1:4-5 (NIV), His life is the light of all mankind and this light shines in the darkness, and the darkness has not overcome it.

We live his life as we manifest his love through our continual love of God our father. The more we love, the more we shine brighter amidst the darkness of this world, and to overcome the darkness so that the spiritually blind may see. For we are the light of the world (Matthew 5:14-16.)

> *You are the light of the world. A town built on a hill cannot be hidden. Neither do people light a lamp and put it under a bowl. Instead they put it on its stand, and it gives light to everyone in the house. In the same way, let your light shine before others, that they may see your good deeds and glorify your Father in heaven.*
> *~ Matthew 5:14-16 New International Version (NIV)*

MAKING WARFARE THROUGH PRAYER FOR THE LOST

The necessity of prayer in soul winning can never be over emphasized. Many renowned soul winners that the world has ever had were giants in prayer. Prayer made them who they were and they made prayer their main stream of liberating and impacting others. Prayer is a God chosen way of partnering with Him to enforce His will on earth. To win and maintain souls at the neglect of prayer is impossible. To achieve what our fore-fathers did in the history of the church with regards to soul winning and prayer, we must consider their ways and do same. (Hebrew 13:7).

> *Remember your leaders, who spoke the word of God to you. Consider the outcome of their way of life and imitate their faith.* ~ *Hebrews 13:7 New International Version (NIV)*

Martin Boos

Before the great revival in Gallneukirchen, said D.M Mcintyre, Martin Boos spent hours, days and nights in the lonely agonies of intercession. Afterwards, when he preached, his words were as flame, and the hearts of the people as grass.

Daniel Nash and Charles Finney

It is said of Daniel Nash (the prayer warrior of Charles Finney), that during the days of great revivals through the crusades of Charles Finney, Pastor Daniel Nash (also famously called Father Nash) would go months or days ahead of Charles Finney to the town where the crusade would be held, rent a room and lock himself in there praying for days. Sometimes, he was found lying prostrate on the floor and groaning without food for days. He would get some prayer men of his caliber to join him. He battled the forces of darkness in the town, prayed for the release of the demonic captives and the entrance of the gospel. This resulted in great harvest of souls during the meetings in places which were ones full of darkness and sin. Nash did not only prepare the communities spiritually for the preaching of the gospel, but he also continued in prayer during the meetings.

Couldn't bend her knee for several months but healed by the power of God at Simbaru, Sierra Leone.

GLMC at Simbaru, Sierra Leone.

While Charles Finney was preaching and after the meetings, he would pray for a list of souls mentioning individual names and making intercession on their behalf, literally in an agony for them. It is said that the meetings of Charles Finney caused liquor shops to close down and for many years crime reduced by as much as 90%.

John Knox

John Knox prayed and said, *"Give me Scotland or I die"*.

John Wesley

John Wesley also said, *"I set my self on fire and people come to watch me burn"*.

Reinhard Bonnke

The recently passed to glory Evangelist Reinhard Bonnke had his crusade meetings backed with many prayer meetings and prayers many days before, during and after the crusade. This led to tremendous results of souls won and souls retained in the faith including many fetish, occults, witches and wizards freed from Satan's power. Many sicknesses, diseases and infirmities inflicted by the devil and even untimely death from the pit of hell were destroyed from the lives of these souls. Many Christians in Africa are a result of these prayers and the preaching of the gospel.

E.M. Bounds once said: speak to God about the people before you speak to the people about God. The prayers of these men brought tremendous results to many receiving the gospel preached to them and receiving salvation through our Lord Jesus Christ. Standing on the believers' authority (Luke 10:19) and victory through the finished works on the cross, they waged war against principalities, powers, the rulers of the darkness of this world, spiritual wickedness in high places (Ephesians 6:12). They waged war against the prince of the power of the air (Ephesians 2:2) who causes disobedience in men and the god of the age (2 Corinthians 4:4) who has blinded and kept men under the power of darkness. They waged war to set the souls of men free to encounter the light of God.

Here are some guidelines, though not exhaustive, to help believers in prayer for souls.

- **Repentance for the people** (2 Chro.7:14, Dan.9:1-20, Ex. 2:1-5, Jonah 3:5-10).
    1. With a heavy and a sincere heart, identify yourself with the resident people at and acknowledge and confess their sins before God (Ps. 32: 4 and 5). Confess the guilt of idolatry, adulatory, witchcraft, high-level occult practices, murder, dishonesty, sexual immoralities, family wickedness, and sinful pleasure of all kind, magical operations, sorcery activities, deception, corruption, and many more that have

given the devil the chance to inflict poverty, hardship and pain over the people.

2. Invoke the atoning power of the blood of Jesus Christ over the individual sins and the sins of the lands in general. By the blood of the Lamb overrule and silence the blood of innocent people (ritual killings, wars) that are crying for vengeance over these lands.

- **Breaking Ancient foundations and Building New Foundation** (Ps.11:1-3, Jer. 1:9-10, Matt.15:13)

1. Break every satanic foundation laid in by the grandfathers and great grandfathers of the lands.

2. Charge the power of the Holy Spirit and the blood of the Lord Jesus against every other foundation established by the blood of animals and humans. Overrule every spoken word that gives root to the evil foundations in the Lands.

3. Renounce and revoke the effect of these foundational negative spirits upon the land and the people –

disunity, poverty, failure, wretchedness, set back, and rebellion.

4. Ask God to lay a new foundation in the lands- a foundation of the fear of the Lord, purity, righteousness, knowledge, unity, prosperity and many more.

- **Dealing with Ancestral Covenants**
  1. Overrule and nullify all covenants, vows, pledges, and agreements made by the founding fathers of our city who covenanted the land and the people to idols and demonic deities, most of which are still presently being worshipped by priest and priestesses.
  2. Revoke all satanic dedications and festivals that covenant the area with deities (earth goddess Diana, Ashera, Baal, Mulech, Appolyon, Mammon, Belial, Paimon, Leviathan, River gods, etc) in the name of Jesus.
  3. By the blood of Jesus overthrow all demonic forces

working behind these covenants.

- **Breaking Satanic Altars** (Isa. 14:24-27, Jer. 51:1-2, Deu.12:3)

  1. Revoke and Break of Curses on the Town
  2. Deal with religious Spirits, satanic gates and barriers against the gospel.
  3. Deal with the principalities, powers, gods, goddesses, witches and the whole satanic hegemony.

- **Pray for the demonstration of the power of God in the lives of the people** (1 Corinthians 2:4-5).

  My message and my preaching were not with wise and persuasive words, but with a demonstration of the Spirit's power, 5 so that your faith might not rest on human wisdom, but on God's power. ~ 1 Corinthians 2:4-5 New International Version (NIV)

- **Pray for the conviction power of the Holy Ghost** (Acts 2:37)

In soul winning we need not only the demonstration of the power of God but even more, we need the conviction power of the Holy Spirit. I have seen many who received miracles go back to their old ways and not surrender to God. I do not understand why yet, but God is sovereign. I have also seen many whose heart are hardened even the more they saw miracles happen. Nonetheless, I am yet to see one person who was deeply convicted by the Holy Spirit and turned back on God. The conviction of the Holy Presence of God brings brokenness and surrender. Even demonic agents surrender their weapons when they experience the convicting presence and power of God. When Apostle Peter spoke, they were deeply cut to the heart by his words being empowered by the Holy Spirit. Thus, they asked what shall we do to be saved? That day, about 3000 souls were saved.

Altar call at Akwamuman, Eastern Region, Ghana

PREACHING THE GOSPEL

After prayer and during prayer we need to take action by preaching the word. For *"How shall they call on Him in whom they have not believed? And how shall they believe in Him of whom they have not heard? And how shall they hear without a preacher? And how shall they preach unless they are sent? As it is written: "How beautiful are the feet of those who preach the gospel of peace, who bring glad tidings of good things!"* (Romans 10:14-15).

How God anointed Jesus of Nazareth with the Holy Spirit and power, and how he went around doing good and healing all who were under the power of the devil—Acts 10:38 (NIV).

We are to go round to go good, preaching the gospel on the highways, the byways, the street corners, the villages, the communities, the towns and the cities till the last man hears the gospel.

ABOUT THE BOOK

Acts 26:17-18 suggests to us our own captivity when we were also lost in our sins and thus, the seriousness of the situation of brethren in our families, clans, villages, communities, towns, cities and nation who do not know the Lord Jesus Christ and have not accepted him as their Lord and Saviour. Following the example of Apostle Paul, we are to submit to Christ, walk in obedience to him in spite of persecution or opposition and do the great commission of going and making disciples of all nations, baptizing them in the name of the Father and of the Son and of the Holy Spirit, and teaching them to obey everything Christ Jesus has commanded us (Mathew 28:19). Let us do the work of an Evangelist as Apostle Paul also admonished his son Timothy (2 Timothy 4:5). Finally, let's have the understanding that soul winning is Spiritual and hence, warfare, and prepare and equip ourselves adequately as our

Lord Jesus Christ who is our captain and army commander leads us in triumphant victories.

Altar call at Nyayanguehun, Sierra Leone

Testifying of various healings at GLMC, Simbaru, Sierra Leone

Altar call at Dawadawa, Brong Ahafo Region, Ghana.

HOW TO PARTNER WITH US

Partner with us to take the gospel to the lost souls in the nations of the world through our Greater Love Miracle Campaigns.

Here are some ways by which you can donate financially to us:

1) E-transfer money to the president (Frederick Amon-Armah: email = famon-armah@hotmail.com),

2) Through PayPal (tfogiom@rocketmail.com, The finger of God International Outreach Ministry)

3) Mobile Money Transfer: 0246055262 (God's Finger Int. Out. Min.)

4) Send to our bank account in Ghana with the information bellow.

    Bank name: Agricultural Development Bank, Ghana.

    Branch: Koforidua,

    Acct name: God's Finger International Outreach Ministry,

    Acct number: 2012000102549403,

    Swift code for international money transfer: ADNTGHAC.

    Ministry address for wire to bank account:
        God's Finger International Outreach Ministry
        P. O. Box KF 2188
        Koforidua
        Eastern Region
        Ghana

www.ingramcontent.com/pod-product-compliance
Lightning Source LLC
Chambersburg PA
CBHW072034060426
42449CB00010BA/2261